BLACK GIRLS UNBOSSED

Young World Changers Leading the Way

KHRISTI LAUREN ADAMS

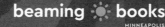

beaming ☀ books
MINNEAPOLIS

For my sister, Chloe, whose leadership
inspires me every single day.

Text copyright © 2022 Khristi Lauren Adams

Published in 2022 by Beaming Books, an imprint of 1517 Media.
All rights reserved. No part of this book may be reproduced
without the written permission of the publisher. Email
copyright@1517.media. Printed in the United States.

Cover illustration and portraits: Aruna Rangarajan
Stock images: Shutterstock Images

28 27 26 25 24 23 22   2 3 4 5 6 7 8

Print ISBN: 978-1-5064-7923-1
eBook ISBN: 978-1-5064-8172-2

Library of Congress Control Number: 2021949527

VN0004589; 9781506479231; FEB2022

Beaming Books
PO Box 1209
Minneapolis, MN 55440-1209
Beamingbooks.com

TABLE OF CONTENTS

INTRODUCTION

Amanda Gorman stepped to the podium with a commanding voice. The National Youth Poet Laureate captured the nation's attention with her inaugural poem, "The Hill We Climb." Journalists marveled at the young poet and activist. "How is she only 22?" one asked. "She reminds me of Maya Angelou," another said. "She's a young hero!" another exclaimed. But there should have been no surprise at Gorman's brilliance. At the same ceremony were Vice President Kamala Harris and Michelle Obama, once young leaders just like Gorman.

Black women and girls have demonstrated their leadership for as long as recorded history. Black girls like Claudette Colvin, who at the age of 15 refused to give up her seat to a white woman on a segregated bus in 1955. Barbara Johns, the 16-year-old who led her classmates in a strike to protest the substandard conditions at her high school in Prince Edward County, Virginia, in 1961. Audrey Faye Hendricks, who, at 9 years old, was the youngest marcher arrested for a civil rights protest in Birmingham, Alabama, in 1963.

Or the 22-year-old college student named Prathia Hall, who in 1962 spoke at a church meeting in Terrell County, Georgia, where Martin Luther King Jr. sat in the audience. At that meeting, she said "I have a dream" repeatedly in a prayer sharing her vision for Black people in America. King was impressed with her speaking skills, and he went on to use this phrase in his famous speech in 1963. Though their stories are often overlooked, Black girls have always played important roles within social movements in the fight for a better and equal world. And Black girls are still leading the way today.

Black girl leaders have emerged from the margins to be the voices of change. These are the young Black women we will be reading about and studying decades from now. The future will be led by Black women and girls.

> # "
>
> # I am a strong believer that there is no age limit on service.
>
> # "

Grace Callwood, Founder and Chairwoman of the We Cancerve Movement, Inc.

HAPPINESS AS HOPE: THE SERVANT LEADERSHIP OF GRACE CALLWOOD

When Grace Callwood was almost 7 years old, her grandmother noticed a lump on her neck. Grace's mother, T'Jae Ellis, scheduled an appointment with a pediatrician and asked about the lump. T'Jae was worried that the lump might be cancer.

The pediatrician didn't listen. She made a racist assumption and told T'Jae that she was braiding Grace's hair too tight. T'Jae tried to tell the doctor that she couldn't be braiding Grace's hair too tightly. But the pediatrician prescribed a cream for the swelling anyway.

T'Jae cried as she drove her daughter to the pharmacy to pick up the cream. At first, she wondered if she was just being paranoid. She was a mother, after all—one whose mind might have gone to the worst-case scenario. But she knew in her gut that something wasn't right. The doctor was missing something important. T'Jae turned out to be right.

One week later, T'Jae noticed a lump on Grace's thigh. They went to another doctor, but this one didn't listen to them either.

T'Jae and Grace met with a third doctor, who finally listened to them and knew something was wrong. A pediatric surgeon took one look at Grace and said she needed to go into surgery.

Grace had a lymph node in her neck removed. Two days later, she was diagnosed with cancer. That night, Grace and her mother

RACIAL BIAS IN
HEALTHCARE

Implicit bias affects Black women's and girls' experiences in the healthcare system. Research has shown that Black women and girls face attitudes and stereotypes that affect the medical care they receive. Grace was the victim of a subconscious stereotype, a doctor's knowledge gap that led to misinformation and a misdiagnosis.

"This is real talk for real women," says T'Jae. "Especially women of color. How many instances do we find ourselves in where we are made to second-guess ourselves and made to feel inadequate or overreacting for things that are legitimately given audience for any other group of people?"

packed their bags to move into the hospital, where Grace would stay for almost two weeks.

It had been two and a half weeks since they first noticed the lump on Grace's neck. If it hadn't been for the persistence of Grace's mother in talking to different doctors, they wouldn't have caught the cancer so quickly. Grace's cancer ultimately went into remission, and she's now 15 years old—but she had been failed by the medical establishment. What if her mother hadn't insisted on getting a second and third opinion? What if she hadn't been skeptical about the doctor's theory and advocated for her daughter? Would they have caught the cancer in time? Would Grace still be alive today?

THE WE CANCERVE MOVEMENT

Today, Grace considers herself much like any other teenage girl. She loves binge-watching Netflix shows with her mother ("I watched *Glee* all the way through—twice," she says, laughing). Grace also has a passion for music. She loves Amy Winehouse, Carole King, The Beatles, Frank Sinatra, and Tony Bennett.

When Grace heard about how happy the girls were to receive the clothes, she knew she wanted to do more.

"I'm in the marching band at my high school," she says. "I play the French horn. I am in the liturgical dance group at my church. I'm also in the youth choir at my church, and of course, community service."

Community service has always been important to Grace, even when she was sick. Since the medicine Grace was taking made her gain and lose weight constantly, she felt she didn't have a need for most of her clothes. She decided to donate them to two girls who had lost their home in a fire. T'Jae delivered the brand new clothes to the girls. When Grace heard about how happy the girls were to receive the clothes, she knew she wanted to do more.

DONATION

Grace was a Wish Kid through the Make-A-Wish Foundation, an organization that "grants life-changing wishes for children with critical illnesses." She had the opportunity to travel to Disney World, where a "gift fairy" distributed gifts to her and the other Wish Kids. After deciding she didn't need the toys, Grace donated them to a local homeless shelter. She also sold lemonade and raised $633 for charity.

One year after her diagnosis, when Grace was only 8 years old, she started an organization that serves some of society's most vulnerable youth.

Today, Grace refers to herself as the "happiness fairy."

The We Cancerve Movement brings "happiness to children experiencing homelessness, illness, or foster care." The name is clever wordplay that transforms the bleakness of the term *cancer* by fusing it with the hopefulness of service.

Grace created a youth-led board of advisors who are all between the ages of 8 and 18. In its very first year, We Cancerve had thirteen board members.

Today, Grace refers to herself as the "happiness fairy." She lights up when she speaks about her organization and its founding. What is often a traumatic time for cancer survivors to think back on—the period when they were at their sickest and their future was most uncertain—Grace remembers as the challenging yet hopeful birth of her movement.

> " I have definitely grown a lot and learned a ton. Starting off, it was just a lot of realizing that I could really make a difference. "

THESE ARE SOME OF WE CANCERVE'S INITIATIVES:

✓ Books & Buddies donates books to help young children pass the hours of infusions during their chemo treatments.

✓ Breakfast Bags Bonanza rallies the community's support to help provide breakfast to children at area homeless shelters and transitional housing programs, foster care group homes and orphanages, local community feeding programs, and Title I schools.

✓ Camp Happy is a free, on-site summer enrichment day camp that includes field trips to local places like dairy farms, movie theaters, swimming pools, and equestrian centers.

✓ **Gift to Give** helps children living at homeless shelters and transitional housing programs give their mothers a gift for Christmas.

✓ **We Cancerve Children's Libraries** provide free books to foster, at-risk, and hospitalized children.

As of 2020, We Cancerve has helped more than **23,000** children and families. Grace channeled what was a life-threatening obstacle into a life-changing movement.

What we can learn from
GRACE CALLWOOD

SERVANT LEADERSHIP

We sometimes think of leaders as people who stand over others, telling them what to do. But Grace shows us what real leadership looks like by serving others. Grace also demonstrates a servant's heart by listening closely to others, having empathy toward them, and working to help promote their healing. How can you demonstrate servant leadership with those around you?

JOY AS ACTIVISM

"I have always loved making people happy," says Grace. She remembers when she was in the hospital fighting cancer, missing school, feeling sick and in pain—but she still felt joy because she could be with her mother. Grace is campaigning for joy and happiness through her service. She calls herself "the happiness fairy," and it is clear that joy is her activism. This joy is part of what led her to create We Cancerve. Where do you find joy, and how can you help share that joy with others?

A SPIRIT OF LEARNING

Grace believes it's important to have a "spirit of learning" when receiving feedback from other people. Leaders need personal awareness and an understanding of the environment and people they serve. Grace allows every moment of her life to be a teachable one. She reflects on how she can learn, grow, and be a better person from every life circumstance she has been presented, whether painful or joyous.

HEALING BY HELPING

Can helping others help us heal ourselves? Grace's story suggests that it can. When Grace had cancer, the surgeries and treatments wiped the strength from her body. But even then, with the little energy she did have, she served. As she gained more strength, she sought to serve even more. Grace kept helping others through her illness. This gave her strength to keep healing—and today, she is cancer-free!

> "The outdoors is not just a place for an individual who looks this way or has these resources. It is a human right."

Amara Ifeji,
Environmental
Justice Activist

SHIFTING THE NARRATIVE:
THE ENVIRONMENTAL ETHICS OF
AMARA IFEJI

2

"I started off exploring in the dirt, and up until I was 18 years old I was still playing in the dirt," Amara Ifeji says, laughing.

In her 18 years, Amara has already made a significant impact as a climate and racial justice activist. A profile piece for a daily Maine newspaper wrote of her prominence, saying, "*As she graduates from Bangor High School, Nigerian-born Amara Ifeji leaves behind a legacy of scientific achievement and social change.*" The article summarized the impact Amara has had in the small corner of the country known as Bangor, Maine.

Amara was born in Nigeria in 2001, and her family moved to the United States in 2004. They first lived in Maryland. When Amara was 9, they moved to Maine.

"I love Maine so much," Amara says. "It has afforded me opportunities. I want to be a part of that progressive change to make the state I love a better place to live, work, and raise a family." However, Amara is disappointed by the slow progress the state has made regarding issues such as racism, equity, and inclusion.

Amara didn't always love Maine. In fact, she spent most of her adolescence wanting to leave the state. Maine is almost 95 percent white. Black people make up less than 2 percent of the population, with other races and ethnicities making up another 2 percent.

Sadly, some of Amara's experiences growing up as a young Black girl in Maine included racism. Two weeks after 9-year-old Amara first moved to the state, she was playing a game on the playground with some of her peers. When she won the game, she was elated. But that excitement faded after a boy called her a racial slur.

As Amara grew up and attended the local school system, she continued to observe racism and discrimination in various forms. She was tired of walking through the halls of her school and hearing the N-word. The racism also extended beyond the school walls.

> **In Maine, there are many sundown towns where I can just really not be found after a certain time. Those are the kinds of things that my mother was fearful of. People who harbored hate for people who look like me.**

Amara wasn't satisfied with leaving things as they were. She optimistically saw herself as a part of the change that she desired to see in Maine. She actively worked to create that change by leading racial advocacy efforts which led to policy change at her school.

Amara has spoken publicly about her experiences for the Bangor City Council and School Committee. One presentation moved to the school board, and she was able to organize the first diversity and inclusion panel discussion at her high school. The panel focused on creating a space to discuss issues of discrimination at her school.

In September 2019, Amara launched the Multicultural Student Union, a group of BIPOC (Black, Indigenous, and People of Color) students who convene once a week to discuss their lived experiences and issues at school. She also founded the Minority Student Union, which aims to bring about change by creating a space for all students to work on developing cultural competence.

Amara's identity as a BIPOC individual living in Maine goes hand-in-hand with her passion for advocating for racial justice. Her passion for environmental issues is also closely linked to her upbringing in Maine, a state of vast forests, wetlands, mountains, and other natural landscapes.

RACISM ON PLAYGROUNDS

Black girls across the country have long been subjected to racism on playgrounds at their schools and in their neighborhoods. The incidents can start unhealthy cycles of self-hatred, and the hurt and humiliation from the incidents can be long-lasting.

"I wasn't embarrassed about what that kid said," Amara says. "I was embarrassed because I was Black. I was embarrassed because I was only one of the three Black kids at my 400-plus elementary school. That started a cycle of me struggling to come to terms with the fact that I am something that is very apparent: Black."

ENVIRONMENTAL ACTIVISM

Though Amara learned about ecosystems and Maine's landscape in school, she didn't receive much environment-focused education. So, she sought out opportunities to educate herself.

While in high school, Amara attended an event with the Maine Environmental Changemakers Association, "a youth-led intergenerational network that connects young Mainers (ages 15–30) from diverse backgrounds who are passionate about the environment with peer mentors, and established professional mentors, in the sector." The event shifted Amara's perspective on the environment from a science-based one to a social one. There, she learned about damage to the environment and the disproportionate impact that this damage has on marginalized communities. Amara also realized that her passions for environmental activism and racial justice were inseparable.

Amara began remembering past experiences that clearly demonstrated a link between the environment and racial and economic injustice. She remembers not being able to afford snow boots and pants, and how this prevented her from connecting with her environment during the winter months. Amara also remembers missing out on environmental outings because of expenses her family was not able to afford. She says that the stigma around Black people skiing or camping also influenced her decision to not engage in those outdoor activities.

Amara also recounts her mother's fear about her going outside, especially at night, because of the danger simply being outside at night can pose to Black people. This evokes the memory of the 2012 murder of 17-year-old Trayvon Martin, who was fatally shot while walking through a neighborhood on his way back from a convenience store. Trayvon was guilty of nothing more than being Black and walking with his hood up in the evening. The fear Black people feel of going outside is another example of an intersectional environmental and social justice issue.

> ❝ **If I did not recognize that there was a link between social justice and environmental issues, I don't really think that I would be in this work. These aren't two different things that I am working towards making better. They are one.** ❞

The overlapping issues Amara speaks of are known as environmental racism. Large segments of the population are disproportionately affected by environmental barriers. Because of this disparity, Amara strives to be a changemaker within the world of environmental activism and environmental equity. She is committed to helping ensure that all people have protection from environmental hazard and access to the environment.

Eventually, Amara evolved from a young woman interested in environmental issues to a climate justice activist. During high school, Amara was involved in the Bangor High School STEM (Science, Technology, Engineering, and Math) program, which tackled issues such as water quality and heavy metal pollution. Amara even participated in an independent research project that focused on the water crisis in Flint, Michigan, by trying to resolve heavy metal contamination in drinking water.

Later, Amara became president of the Stormwater Management and Research Team (SMART). SMART is a "youth-led water quality management team which aims to provide female students with opportunities to explore environmental STEM."

ENVIRONMENTAL **EQUITY**

Land is a source of livelihood, providing essential food and water. For Black people, land is also an important part of our historical identity and spirituality. Our African ancestors believed land was a gift from God. Because of this, they took great pride in the land and saw themselves as stewards of God's resources. Unfortunately for Black Americans, slavery forced our ancestors to work the land and build the infrastructure of America with sweat and blood and no reward.

Amara explains, "Those who are typically affected by things like natural disasters and environmental phenomena are BIPOC individuals. Especially when one of three African American individuals lives within thirty miles (forty-eight kilometers) of a coal plant."

For her work in environmental justice, Amara was awarded the Maine Environmental Education Association Student of the Year Award. Her research projects, which have won numerous awards, centered on methods of water purification.

Amara's dedication to intersectional environmentalism led her to become a Grassroots Development Coordinator with the Maine Environmental Changemakers Association. In this role, Amara continues to advocate for intersectional climate justice solutions through various programs and initiatives.

> " **Through my work, I've led efforts to allow individuals, especially those from marginalized backgrounds, to recognize that the environment and the outdoors is not just a place for an individual who looks this way or has these resources. It is a human right.** "

Amara Ifeji continues that legacy of Black Americans returning to the land by teaching that we all have an ethical responsibility to protect its sacredness.

What we can learn from
AMARA IFEJI

ETHICAL LEADERSHIP

An ethical leader is guided by their values, beliefs, and principles. They respect and serve others, are honest, and work to build community. Amara has a clear code of ethics, one that celebrates inclusivity and justice. What is your code of ethics? How can you be an ethical leader in your community?

CONSTRUCTIVE CRITICISM

Amara loves her community dearly. Because of this love, she was keenly aware there were things she wanted to change. Amara's criticism didn't come from an intent to cause harm, but from a desire to see something she loved become even better. We can be critical of the things we love when we include truth and ethics in our critique.

EVERYONE BELONGS

Amara not only believes everyone has a place in the outdoors, but also believes everyone has a place in our society at large. Amara strives to be inclusive of all individuals in all communities. What can you do to be more welcoming of others around you?

DEFINE YOUR OWN STORY

Amara experienced discrimination throughout her childhood. This treatment affected the way she saw herself. But Amara learned to reject the negative stories others were using to define her, and she created her own story. Amara learned to define herself, as well as the meaning of identity, in her own terms. By the time she graduated from high school, she stood out in a different way, making an extraordinary name for herself in Maine and beyond.

> **"Frankly, we just need to get okay with being not okay. We need to accept our flaws and love ourselves no matter what."**
>
> *Hannah Lucas, notOK App Founder and Developer*

LOOKING TO THE FUTURE: THE VISION OF

HANNAH LUCAS

3

One evening when Hannah Lucas's mother was getting ready for bed, she stopped at the top of the stairs to check on her daughter. She knew 15-year-old Hannah had been facing bullying and harassment at school, and that she was warding off depression and despair. But Hannah's mother didn't know how deep that despair was, nor that her daughter believed there was only one way to escape the unbearable pain.

Hannah's mother opened the bedroom door just as Hannah was putting a handful of pills into her mouth. She ran over to her daughter, grabbed her, and took the pills out of her mouth. At that moment Hannah said, "I don't want to be here anymore. I can't take it anymore." Then she said something that would change the course of her life and many others': "I just wish there was a button I could press!"

In that moment of desperation and anguish, Hannah had a vision.

With the help of her mother, Hannah survived the night and lived to share her experience. Now, Hannah helps others who find themselves in the same state of hopelessness.

Hannah Lucas is a survivor with a story to tell.

For most of her childhood, Hannah was a competitive gymnast. But shortly after leaving the sport, she began to experience symptoms of a chronic illness. It all started with severe headaches. Over time, the illness worsened. One day, the school nurse called Hannah's mother to tell her Hannah had passed out. Eventually, Hannah began passing out almost every day, and her mother would have to pick her up from school.

Doctors could not figure out what was wrong with Hannah. While they were concerned, some doctors didn't believe the things Hannah told them about her symptoms.

Remember Grace Callwood and her mother, T'Jae? Grace's pediatrician had brushed off T'Jae's concerns, making assumptions about the braiding of Grace's hair instead of seriously examining the swelling which turned out to be cancer. Hannah's experience—as a Black teenage girl being misdiagnosed by white medical professionals—is one case in the larger story of Black girls' and women's health and medical outcomes being endangered by a medical establishment that's not designed for them.

Hannah received several different—and conflicting—diagnoses. Eventually, she was diagnosed with Postural Orthostatic Tachycardia Syndrome, or POTS, an autonomic nervous system disorder that affects blood circulation.

As a result of her illness, Hannah became a victim of extreme bullying, harassment, and threats in high school.

> **I would hear people talking about me—and I would be standing right behind them—saying, 'Yeah this girl is so weird, she has seizures.'**

MENTAL **HEALTH**

One in four people worldwide struggle mentally or emotionally, and suicide is the second leading cause of death in youth ages 13 to 24. Fifty-four percent of people who died by suicide did not have a mental health diagnosis. Many factors can put a person at risk of suicide, including family history of suicide, substance abuse, chronic illness, prolonged stress, and isolation. If you or someone you know needs help, call the National Suicide Prevention Lifeline at **800-273-TALK**.

Hannah was a good student, and also the only Black girl in her class. She believes that's why she was the victim of bullying. In addition to making fun of her illness, white students would make fun of her hair and say the N-word around her.

Even though she had been an honors student, Hannah began having a difficult time making it through her classes. Her illness resulted in brain fog. Between that and the increase in bullying, she struggled. By the end of her first year of high school, Hannah had missed 196 classes due to her condition.

Hannah's depression got worse, which led her to struggle with disordered eating. She would go days without eating and then binge eat until she vomited. From there, she began to self-harm. She began to bleach her skin to try to get lighter.

Hannah's mother knew her daughter was struggling; she just didn't know the depths of her emotional struggle. "I witnessed her completely just wither away every single day. Her light just dimmed," Hannah's mother recalled.

Hannah's tipping point was the guilt she felt about the toll her illness, the bullying, and the resulting depression had taken on her loved ones. Not only did she have her own pain, but she also couldn't help but feel like she was the source of her mother's pain.

After years of battling depression, Hannah decided that the only way to ease both of their pain would be to die by suicide.

> **That night, my mom saved my life. When she was holding me, I just remember my thumb.**

That night, Hannah understood that others who are in emotional, mental, or physical distress may not be as fortunate as she was to have someone there to help save them. In her moment of despair, Hannah had a vision of herself pressing an app on her phone with her thumb. She imagined a digital panic button someone in need could use to call out to a loved one for help.

> **❝ I just wanted something that I could physically press that wasn't a life alarm necklace. I just remember wanting an app on my phone that I could press. ❞**

A little over a week after the incident, Hannah could not get the idea of the app out of her head. She realized that, if she were ever in that position again, she wanted certain people to know she was not okay, and she wanted them to know where to find her. For Hannah, it would be something that she could use for both her mental illness and her chronic illness. She knew this vision would benefit not only herself, but also others who found themselves in a similar position.

When Hannah's research determined that an app like that didn't exist, she told her 12-year-old brother, Charlie, about her vision. Charlie had taught himself how to build apps and programs at 7 years old, so he already had the basic skills to help realize Hannah's vision.

Once Charlie was done with the preliminary programming, the siblings created a fifteen-page presentation about the app to demonstrate to their parents that they were serious about the endeavor. Then they found developers to help. While Charlie worked on refining the app, Hannah worked on the business side, helping to secure an LLC and deciding how to best market the app. She also entered into intensive therapy and life coaching to help with her mental health.

When it was time to launch the app, Hannah and Charlie named it notOK—because, as their slogan says, "It's okay to be notOK."

The notOK app is a digital panic button that, when pressed,

sends an alert to up to five of the user's pre-selected contacts to let them know the user is not okay. The app automatically sends out the distressed person's current GPS location and directions. Currently, the app has more than 70,000 users. Users have hit the notOK button at least 50,000 times.

> In our society, there remains a stigma around asking for help; according to Hannah, we should normalize seeking help.

The website for notOK lists Hannah, Charlie, and their dog Trooper (whose responsibilities are listed as "emotional support and encouragement") as part of the notOK team. The website also lists important facts about mental health. It includes information about support groups and resources for those struggling with mental health issues, alongside the option to download other apps.

Since the app's launch, Hannah has emerged as a spokesperson for Black women's mental health. She and Charlie have been invited to speak and interview at events and organizations. Hannah attributes part of the app's appeal to the fact that it takes the guesswork out of asking for help. In our society, there remains a stigma around asking for help; according to Hannah, we should normalize it.

Hannah's app draws us one step closer to normalizing seeking help. And the app's users are grateful it exists. One user wrote,

★★★★★

"This app alerted my mom that I was not ok and she showed up very fast."

Another said,

★★★★★

"Sometimes when I'm having a panic attack, I can't sit and text—from shaking—or I just can't think clearly. This app makes it easy to let people know you're NOT ok and you need help."

Still another user wrote:

★★★★★

"Such a great app to save lives!"

Hannah and Charlie—and Trooper the dog—are doing just that. They are in the business of saving lives.

What we can learn from
HANNAH LUCAS

VISIONARY LEADERSHIP

In one of the most difficult moments in her life, Hannah Lucas had a vision. She not only saw herself pressing a button that would save her life, but also envisioned other people in a similar position who would one day use that button to save their own lives. Hannah is part of a long ancestral line of Black women visionary leaders. Women like Harriet Tubman, Dorothy Height, Shirley Chisholm, and Oprah Winfrey are just a few Black women whose visions helped positively change society and influence the world. Can you imagine the future you want to create?

IT'S OKAY TO NOT BE OKAY

While we know perfection is unattainable, images of perfection have become part of our identities, especially on social media. As a result, it's difficult to be vulnerable enough to share our imperfect moments. Many of us do not feel safe to do so. Chasing perfection can lead to feeling like we always have to have it together. The entire premise of the notOK app is that it is okay to not be okay. It is okay to be disappointed. It is okay to be hurt. It is okay to not have things figured out. It is okay to feel lost. We must accept that it is okay to not be okay and to feel whatever we feel when life gets hard.

IT'S OKAY TO BE UNIQUE

It's okay to be unique. Uniqueness is being unlike anything or anyone else. Every individual has something unique about them, whether it's in their physicality or their personality. God designed our makeup with intention and gave us all permission to be unique. Hannah demonstrates that our uniqueness should not be hidden away. Our individuality is one of the greatest assets we can offer this world. You are the only one of you in the world.

IT'S OKAY TO LOVE YOURSELF

Self-love sounds like a simple concept, but it proves difficult for many people. This is because it requires ignoring or removing the harmful stigmas of outside influences. Oftentimes, outside voices and opinions can have tremendous effects on our self-worth. However, it is our opinions of ourselves that matter most. "Learn how to love every single aspect of you," Hannah advises. "Learn how to love the very essence of yourself, and then it'll make whatever you do in life that much easier because you won't care about how people perceive you."

> "I want to make Brown Kids Read a big thing to show kids that a Black girl can do this and that Black girls are important enough to be featured in literature.

Ssanyu Lukoma,
Founder of Brown Kids Read

BORN WITH A PURPOSE: THE STRATEGIC THINKING OF

SSANYU LUKOMA

4

Ssanyu Lukoma taught herself to read when she was barely 4 years old. At age 5, she fell in love with a book called *Rosa*, an inspiring children's book about Rosa Parks, written by poet, activist, and educator Nikki Giovanni. The story is about the day Parks refused to give up her seat for a white person on a segregated bus and how this event sparked the famous 1955 Montgomery, Alabama, bus boycotts. The book explores Parks' life and activism while also highlighting other women who made the movement possible.

Ssanyu fell in love with the story and liked to imagine that if she had been in Parks' position, she would have made the same decision. Even at that young age, Ssanyu's passion for reading set the foundation for her leadership.

Ssanyu is homeschooled and enjoys the freedom and flexibility that comes with it. At the same time, she is a social person and misses being with her friends during the school day. Ssanyu's favorite subject is literature, or anything having to do with reading and writing. "Books create so many pathways," she says.

Ssanyu is a proud member of the New Jersey Orators, a youth organization where she does competitive public speaking, and KiDz HuB Media Network, a nonprofit that trains and mentors youth as junior broadcasters and journalists. She is also the proud older sibling to a brother and sister. Ssanyu works to better herself as a leader for them. In a time when unarmed Black people are being shot by police officers, violent white supremacy is at work, and gun ownership and mass shootings are on the rise, she worries for her siblings' safety.

> **All the things going on like school shootings and Black men being killed in the street, it hurts. I get scared. My little brother is 9. I don't want him to walk outside and be scared that he's going to be holding a bag of candy and somebody is going to come and attack him just because of the color of his skin.**

When young Black boys and girls are exposed to this trauma, the consequences are distrust, grief, and at times, paralyzing fear. For comfort and strength, Ssanyu turns to her faith in God. Ever since she was young, she and her family have been active in their local church.

"I feel like God placed me in that environment so that I was able to feel like nothing can stop me," she says. Ssanyu sees God in the relationships she has built at church.

"In Sunday school, we were just studying the scripture, 'For I know the plans I have for you, plans to prosper you and not to harm you, plans to give you hope and a future.' That really touched me," she says. "When I feel like I want to give up, I know that it hurts God when I have those thoughts because He gave me talent and He gave me gifts and He gave me a special purpose to do these things. And that's why I keep pushing and I keep going."

This persistence—and her commitment to use the gifts that God has given her—has propelled Ssanyu to one of her greatest achievements: founding the organization Brown Kids Read.

DIVERSITY IN LITERATURE

#OwnVoices is a hashtag that started on Twitter where people recommend books about diverse characters written by BIPOC authors. The movement highlights the importance of representation by diverse authors. The hashtag initially focused on calling attention to diversity in children's literature but has since expanded to all literature. Recently, the movement shifted focus when We Need Diverse Books discontinued using #OwnVoices in favor of the descriptions authors use for themselves and their characters.

BROWN KIDS READ

Ssanyu was 12 years old when she got the idea for her organization. "The first time I thought of Brown Kids Read, it wasn't supposed to be an organization," Ssanyu says. "It was just supposed to be a partnership with another nonprofit to do a fundraiser for them."

The nonprofit, called Double Dose, was led by Ssanyu's friends, twins who had written a book together. At the time, Ssanyu was working with another author to turn the author's book into a party entertainment business. They were developing a plan where Ssanyu would dress up as the book's main character and produce story time packages to sell to parents and teachers for children's parties.

When Ssanyu heard that Double Dose was doing an event at a Barnes & Noble bookstore, she pitched the idea of partnering with the twins for the party entertainment venture. Ssanyu also thought it would be good to solicit other authors to do signings.

> **We needed a name for it, since Barnes & Noble asks for the name of your event . . . so we came up with Brown Kids Read. Once I got to that event and I saw the kids buying the books and I saw the excitement on their faces, I was like, 'I want to replicate this.'**

Ssanyu realized that a lot of the kids in her age group did not have the opportunity to read and learn about diverse literature. Her Black and brown peers didn't have ready access to books written by people of color—children's and young adult books that center the perspectives and agency of characters of color.

In an effort to make Brown Kids Read more appealing to kids, Ssanyu built on the concept of bringing books to life. While registering Brown Kids Read as an official 501(c)(3) organization, Ssanyu put on a series of community reading events. The organization's nonprofit status became official in November 2018. By the beginning of 2019, Ssanyu—with the help of her parents—had put on a series of community reading events. But she was starting to realize how difficult it is to get kids out to read.

From there, Ssanyu came up with the concept of a pop-up bookstore: a traveling book display she could take to local events. Her parents loaned her $2,000 to purchase books, and she began setting up the Brown Kids Read pop-up bookstore to display and sell books at various events.

Soon, organizations began to contact Ssanyu for interviews, to support her work, and to help get the word out about her organization. Brown Kids Read now offers a host of events throughout the year.

Ssanyu continues to promote the importance of diverse books for youth through various Brown Kids Read initiatives.

Along with its community reading events, Brown Kids Read offers books for sale through its website; the main page features a diverse array of illustrated brown faces on the covers. The website also sells merchandise such as tote bags, journals, T-shirts, and travel mugs.

Brown Kids Read even offers young people the opportunity to read and review books of their choosing on the site.

In addition to selling books and merchandise, Ssanyu also writes book reviews for the diverse literature she promotes on her website. Brown Kids Read even offers young people the opportunity to review books on the site. And from time to time, the organization holds essay-writing contests for youth, with the opportunity to win cash prizes and other gifts.

Ssanyu is serious about the work she does and the young people she serves through her organization. She wants the kids she serves to be excited about books, and she believes that representation of diverse voices is the gateway to that excitement.

Ssanyu is focused and prepared for her future, fully able to handle whatever comes next for herself and for Brown Kids Read.

> **God gave me purpose. My purpose is to lead. My purpose is to inspire people. I've come to the realization that I don't want to be the next Oprah. I want to be the first Ssanyu.**

What we can learn from
SSANYU LUKOMA

PROBLEM-SOLVING

Ssanyu is a problem-solver. She prides herself on her ability to think critically. She reflects on all of her endeavors, thinking about what she can do better next time. Any time she has faced challenges, she considers them teachable moments to grow. "I am very good at seeing the logic in situations," she says, "so I'm always trying to figure out what's the most efficient way to do something or how we can solve a problem quickly." How are you a problem-solver in your everyday life?

STRATEGIC LEADERSHIP

Ssanyu had a vision, created goals, and set up a plan. Strategic leaders create structures that equip their organizations to achieve their goals. They also consistently think about their organizations' long- and short-term successes. It's important to have a vision, but it's also essential to have a plan for that vision. What is your vision, and have you set up a plan to make sure it comes to life?

MORAL LEADERSHIP

Ssanyu's approach to her business is rooted in the calling she believes God has given her. This way of thinking is rooted in a history of Black women who connect their religious and spiritual duties to their social responsibilities. For Ssanyu, fulfilling her moral obligation means using the gifts that God gave her to address a pressing social need. "Why would God give me this if I was just supposed to give up?" she asks.

TENACITY

A scripture passage says that faith unaccompanied by action is useless (James 2:17). One translation says it this way: "Faith without works is dead." As a young woman of faith, Ssanyu believes that her faith must be supported by work. "God is never going to just hand things to you," she says. "You have to work for it. If you just give up, then what is that saying to God? That you're not going to use the talent that He gave you?" To Ssanyu, it is not enough to have talent; we must use our gifts and work for the goals that we seek to attain in life.

> "Black women are literally the helm of every movement. Every push for social justice. Every push for social change. We need to take our stories into our own hands."

Tyah-Amoy Roberts,
Activist

MARCHING FOR BLACK LIVES: THE TRANSFORMING ACTIVISM OF

TYAH-AMOY ROBERTS

"There was just a shooting at your high school."
Tyah-Amoy Roberts looked down at the text message from her mother in disbelief. It had only been a few minutes since her mother had dropped Tyah off at a local community college to attend a class that was part of an accelerated program for high school students. Tyah disregarded the message, thinking that it was just a drill and her mother got the wrong information.

Still, something told her to look online to see if it was true. It was. When she found information confirming the incident, Tyah became concerned.

On February 14, 2018, a teenage gunman opened fire with a semiautomatic rifle at Marjory Stoneman Douglas High School (MSD) in Parkland, Florida. Claiming the lives of seventeen people and injuring many others, it was the deadliest high school shooting to date in United States history.

At the time, Tyah was in her junior year at the school. She had left the building less than twenty minutes before the shooting occurred. While she was physically removed from the situation, the emotional devastation left her helpless.

5

> **"** I was calling my friends and they weren't answering, and I was so scared. I was soaked in tears so much that my dress was messed up. **"**

Tyah felt a lot of internal tension: gratitude and relief that she was not at the school at the time, but also the feeling that she should have been there with her friends and classmates.

Tyah was supposed to give a speech that day in her class at the college. Her teacher told her that she could be excused. But Tyah told the teacher she wanted to give her presentation despite her anguish—foreshadowing how she would later channel pain from the tragedy into transformative speaking.

In the days and weeks following the shooting, Tyah attended funeral after funeral while still attending school and trying to move forward with the rest of her peers. She had a difficult time processing what had taken place.

GUN
CONTROL

A little over five years before the shooting at MSD, a gunman killed twenty-six people at Sandy Hook, a Connecticut elementary school. Twenty of the victims were children between 6 and 8 years old.

Time magazine found that between the Sandy Hook shooting in 2012 and the Parkland shooting in 2018, there had been sixty-three high school shootings in the United States. Many people thought the tragedy of an elementary school massacre would spark significant change in gun control policy in the United States. Though many state laws have been passed, major attempts at federal legislation have failed.

March for Black Lives

Tyah doesn't remember Sandy Hook or most other school shootings, though she does recall a few leading up to the MSD incident. She never considered that such a thing could take place at her own school.

Several years after the shooting at her high school, Tyah became a student at Stanford University. There is no doubt her life transformed after February 14, 2018. Yet through it all, she reached through depths of pain and emerged as a voice for change.

Initially after the MSD shooting, national attention focused on the school and surviving students. Some of those survivors sought counseling and formed support groups. Some found comfort in what remained of normal life, spending time with friends and attending classes. Others turned their grief and anger into activism.

A little over a month after the tragedy, *Time* magazine did a cover story on five survivor-activists at the forefront of the gun control conversation. Those five activists were Jaclyn Corin, X González, David Hogg, Cameron Kasky, and Alex Wind. To the public, they had become the faces representing MSD survivors.

None of those faces, however, were Black. At the time, MSD was about 25 percent Black. But outsiders would not know that from how the media depicted the school.

Tyah and her friend and classmate Mei-Ling Ho-Shing were frustrated about the way the media was ignoring the Black students who were also speaking out against gun violence. They decided to host a press conference about feeling silenced as members of the MSD Black community.

The press conference took place just a few days after the March for Our Lives rally, a student-led demonstration in Washington, DC, that brought attention to gun violence and promoted gun legislation. A school board member helped the Black high school students get in touch with local news media and other important community members to attend the press conference.

Tyah and the group wanted to use their media attention to highlight other Black communities that were being ignored.

Tyah and the group wanted to use their media attention to highlight other Black communities that were being ignored. After their initial press conference, the students began making contact with other schools in Black communities to offer support.

Meanwhile, the Black students at MSD continued to be overlooked. Tyah shared her frustration with one of the student-activists publicly on Twitter. Shortly after, X González—though not the recipient of the original tweet—texted Tyah and asked if she wanted to go on a "Road for Change" trip with them. This was how Tyah got started working with March for Our Lives.

Tyah went on the road with the other students the summer before her senior year. The experience was exciting. Tyah sat on panels, and she also gave a lot of speeches, which she enjoyed. Because of her success as a speaker, Tyah stayed with the organization after the tour.

Tyah began flying all over the country, giving speeches at various events. Her speeches usually focused on reminding audiences to support Black communities. Tyah's busy speaking schedule took place over most of her senior year, and she struggled to manage both her travel and schoolwork.

During this time, Tyah also became an ambassador for the United State of Women, a national organization dedicated to the fight for gender equity. Tyah mainly worked on the topic of women of color and equity. She also worked with the Brady Campaign to Prevent Gun Violence. The organization is named after Jim and Sarah Brady, who dedicated their lives to advocating for common-sense gun laws at the state and federal level.

By the end of her senior year, Tyah was a board member for March for Our Lives.

By the end of her senior year, Tyah was a board member for March for Our Lives. At the same time, she was working two jobs to save money for college. In her first few months at Stanford University that fall, Tyah stayed busy with her responsibilities for March for Our Lives. But eventually, she stepped back from some of her organizational responsibilities so she could focus on her schoolwork. However, Tyah remains an advocate for Black women leaders.

Tyah challenges, inspires, and motivates. Through her work, she asks her counterparts: What kind of a society are you creating through your philosophies and actions? How are you incorporating the voices of the marginalized through your work? Tyah adamantly rejects any vision for a society that excludes Black leadership and livelihood.

Tyah remains focused on what she perceives as her life's calling. Like all transformational leaders whose focus is on motivating people to reach their individual potential, Tyah wants Black girls to know they can do whatever they want to do and be whoever they want to be.

When asked what wakes her up in the morning and gets her doing all the work she does, Tyah replies,

> **Black girls. One hundred percent. That's the reason why I do literally anything ever. I want Black girls to feel like, 'She's doing it, so I can too.'**

What we can learn from
TYAH-AMOY ROBERTS

TRANSFORMATIONAL LEADERSHIP

Real leadership helps transform people's hearts, minds, and actions by holding people to a higher standard. The transformation that happens is a result of individuals who have been inspired to achieve collective goals. Transformational leaders like Tyah engage with others and create a connection. This leadership energizes and motivates people, inspiring them toward a shared vision.

AUTHENTICITY

Tyah believes that the opportunities she has been afforded in life have happened because of her diligence and commitment to stand for what is right and just. In a society that sometimes encourages changing oneself to fit in socially, being one's truest, most authentic self is a form of resistance.

LIVE BY EXAMPLE

Tyah feels like the best thing she has done in her life is be an example. Our core beliefs and values must be practiced in front of others, because we may be the only sacred text that someone else ever reads. This is the responsibility we have to others. We must live not just for ourselves, but with the mind that our actions could influence someone else for good or bad.

PRIORITIZE MENTAL HEALTH

Tyah doesn't have many regrets in life, but one thing that does give her unease is the lack of attention she gave to her mental health following the tragedy at her school. There is a general sentiment that Black women and girls should be able to handle anything, even beyond the weight that humans should carry alone. But we know that we are allowed to be vulnerable and fragile, even in our strength. It's okay to need help and to seek it out.

> # " Being able to use my platform for something that is so much bigger than me is so amazing. "

Jaychele Nicole Schenck, Cofounder and Executive Director of Gen Z: We Want to Live

JAYCHELE NICOLE SCHENCK

6

"People are paying attention now! They are listening to us now whether they want to or not! They have no choice but to sit at home and watch us or be here and protest with us or fight with us!"

Jaychele Nicole Schenck shouted these words into a bullhorn as people surrounded her, clapping and cheering in agreement. Her leadership had brought more than 1,500 people to the Rhode Island State House lawn in Providence to protest injustices against Black men and women in the United States. The protest came after the tragic murder of George Floyd sparked a national outcry.

On a Sunday in June 2020, the gatherers marched from Burnside Park to the state house. The group then staged a "die-in," lying down as if dead in the streets outside Providence Place Mall. They lay on the ground for eight minutes and forty-six seconds, the amount of time a Minneapolis police officer knelt on the neck of George Floyd, ultimately causing his death.

"Black Lives Matter!" Jaychele exclaimed to the crowd, a sea of multiethnic and intergenerational faces. The crowd shouted the same phrase back repeatedly as people raised signs and held up cell phones to capture the moment in pictures and videos.

Jaychele was bold and passionate and shouted as though her life depended on the words coming out of her mouth. They reflected the sentiment behind Gen Z: We Want to Live, the organization that Jaychele and cofounder Isabella James Indellicati started.

> **I started thinking, what are things that Gen Z'ers all have in common? We all have dealt with tragedies like school shootings and race-based violence, climate change. What do we want to do? We all want to live. We ended up piecing it all together: Gen Z: We Want to Live.**

Jaychele's thrust into activism began after one of these tragic moments for Gen Z youth. She was in the eighth grade when the mass shooting at Marjory Stoneman Douglas High School in Parkland, Florida, occurred. The gunman killed seventeen people and injured many others. In the aftermath of the shooting, Jaychele saw the young leaders who emerged from the tragedy, and she was immediately inspired. She later attended a March for Our Lives rally in Rhode Island, and she felt compelled to testify.

Jaychele explains that testifying, in the realm of social activism, is speaking about an important issue at a public hearing. "Testifying is normally when you are speaking about a bill. It is usually related to the law," she says.

Before Jaychele could testify, she wanted to learn how to be a good public speaker. In the ninth grade, she joined Young Voices. This organization focuses on community and policy work. Jaychele credits Young Voices for her initial leadership training through their workshops and programs. One program, called Hotshots, taught public speaking.

In her time with Young Voices, Jaychele gravitated toward policy work and focused mainly on gun control.

> **" I started off doing minor community building, and from there I really became an activist. "**

At a 2019 "Wear Orange" event—aimed at gun violence—in Providence, Jaychele recited a poem she'd written.

As a youth, I have been told that activism is a hobby

As a youth, I have been told that I am not capable of influencing policy

As a youth, I have been told that gun violence is a grown-up issue

As a youth, I have been told to let the adults continue

As a youth, I have been told to wait my turn

And now it is my turn to be a thorn

In the side of the politicians that fail to realize

The sounds of the cries from the parents getting the phone call that their children have died . . .

Young Voices also provided what Jaychele described as "community circles." When a national crisis occurred, community circles provided students with a safe space to talk. Jaychele grew within the organization; at 13 years old, she became a board member and was involved with event planning and fundraising.

Jaychele attended high school at the Metropolitan Regional Career and Technical Center in Rhode Island. She was a math genius, skipping Algebra 2 and Geometry; she took college-level math her junior year. Jaychele finished high school with an associate's degree from attending an accelerated program. Harvard, Yale, and Brown University were some of her top choices for college.

Jaychele is inspired by other Black women leaders, including Stacey Abrams. "She is such an inspiration to me," Jaychele says. "She's such a huge personality in the best way possible and for the best reasons. Her presence speaks for her. She is so inspiring that whenever people see her or see what she has done, they immediately have a feeling of jumping into action."

STACEY **ABRAMS**

Voting rights activist, lawyer, and politician Stacey Abrams is known as the woman who helped Georgia turn blue in the 2020 presidential election. Abrams spent more than ten years fighting against voter suppression in Georgia. Her organization, Fair Fight, worked to raise awareness about voter suppression, educate people of color on voting rights, and create voter protection teams across the state. Through her mobilization efforts, she helped register more than 800,000 new voters in Georgia.

GEN Z: WE WANT TO LIVE

Jaychele and Gen Z's other cofounder, Isabella, first connected on social media through a mutual friend. They had similar interests, one being their desire to bring attention to the nation's social injustices. They were planning a protest event with another group, but circumstances caused them to pull out of the protest. That led them to brainstorm about creating something on their own.

> While adult guidance has been beneficial, Jaychele makes it clear that Gen Z: We Want to Live is youth led.

The nonprofit's mission is to fight for Gen Z "through youth advocacy and political influence, by building a coalition of skilled young activists." While adult guidance has been beneficial, Jaychele makes it clear that Gen Z: We Want to Live is youth led.

Jaychele and Isabella started the organization on June 1, 2020. They announced their first protest on June 9, and five days later, 1,500 people gathered for their protest. They used their built-in social media followings for engagement and marketing.

On June 22, the organization's website announced its first batch of policy initiatives. They included implementing culturally relevant curriculums in the education system, diversifying the education workforce, and putting police through independent training and racial bias testing.

In an email to supporters on July 11, Jaychele wrote: *"I am not just fighting for myself. I am fighting for the thousands of communities and millions of girls like me that are currently impacted and will continue to be without your support . . .. The youth are counting on you."*

No words could ring truer. Young Black girl leaders like Jaychele are counting on us and we cannot let them down.

Of her future, Jaychele says she wants to run for state senate while she's in college, with plans to run for US Senate by the time she is 30.

" There are currently no Black women in the Senate, and I want to run. "

We hope, however, that by the time Jaychele arrives, she will be welcomed into the company of other Black women Senate leaders who will help usher us all into a new era of change.

What we can learn from

JAYCHELE NICOLE SCHENCK

MOBILIZING LEADERSHIP

Black women have been at the forefront of mobilizing for years, and Jaychele is one such leader. She motivates and organizes in the fight against oppression. She orients and focuses the attention of others. Mobilizing leaders show us that activism and resistance can come in different forms. What can you do to organize and mobilize those around you for a worthy cause?

BELIEF IN WHAT YOU'RE FIGHTING FOR

Jaychele believes in the ability of her generation to make our world a better place. She believes in what she fights for. Believing in what you fight for can help sustain you as you work to bring truth and change to the world around you. It is not enough to fight; we must also continually revisit the reason why we fight. What is your why?

IT'S OKAY TO GET EMOTIONAL

Jaychele is unapologetically emotional about the causes she cares deeply about. She knows anger is part of the work, and she's not afraid of her emotions. Instead of shying away from the "angry Black woman" trope, Jaychele has found a way to lean into it. Acknowledge that your anger is real, justified, and human. And use those emotions to create change.

STRIVE FOR A HIGHER SELF

"I believe in God, but I also tend to focus on my higher self," Jaychele says. In order to connect to the divine essence that God placed in us, our focus must turn inward. All of us should strive to become the best versions of ourselves; but to do so, we must commit to doing internal work.

> " **Art is life and we learn from and adapt to it.** "

*Kynnedy Simone Smith,
Scholar, Violinist, and
Entrepreneur*

THE HERO OF HER OWN STORY: THE PACESETTING OF

KYNNEDY SIMONE SMITH

7

Before Kynnedy Simone Smith was even born, her mother declared that she would be the child to break generational curses in their family. Although Kynnedy's mother would raise her as a single parent in difficult financial and personal circumstances, she dedicated her life to ensuring Kynnedy had every resource she needed to thrive.

This love, sacrifice, and hard work paid off. Seventeen-year-old Kynnedy is an academic scholar, a classically trained violinist, and the founder of several initiatives and organizations. She has received multiple honors and awards, and she is passionate about STEM, the arts, and matters of diversity and inclusion.

At Kynnedy's predominately white independent school, there have been times when people told her to stop talking because her accomplishments made them feel bad. "It is a lot of pressure, but it's all good pressure. But it did fuel in me a sense of perfectionism at a young age. Every day I am always being told that I need to be five times better than everyone else, especially as a Black female."

Originally from Shaker Heights, Ohio, Kynnedy grew up surrounded by Cleveland arts and culture. She took dance, music, and art classes all throughout her childhood.

Kynnedy was gifted her first violin by her local Boys & Girls Club when she was in the fourth grade. That gift began a journey that started with Kynnedy joining her elementary school orchestra. She is now a gospel jazz violinist with more than ten years of classical and contemporary music study. She has performed on both national and international stages. She goes by Kynnedy Simone as her performance name. In the future, she wants to be a session musician, performing for recording sessions.

> **I want music to continue to be something that I do for enjoyment and for healing purposes. I'm really big on music for healing.**

At Kynnedy's school, she is on the volleyball team, in the string ensemble, and on the speech and debate team. She is also a founding member of the Black Student Union and a member of the Diversity Club and Multicultural Club.

In 2019, Kynnedy was invited to attend Disney Dreamers Academy. She calls the experience "one of the most life-changing things that ever happened to me." Kynnedy was chosen as one of one hundred distinguished teens to engage in the transformational and intensive four-day leadership program hosted by the Steve & Marjorie Harvey Foundation, *Essence* magazine, and Walt Disney World.

Kynnedy recalls the experience fondly; being surrounded by so many accomplished Black people was transformative for her. She realized that if she could put the work in and take advantage of the abundant community, "literally anything would be possible." But Kynnedy also thought about why everyone didn't have access to such an experience. That's when she formed the mission for her organizations.

I ART CLEVELAND

Kynnedy was just 11 years old when she started her first nonprofit organization, I Art Cleveland.

"I started I Art Cleveland because art saved my life," Kynnedy says. "I'm not sure I would be here without art. Art created me into the leader I am today, and I want to use art in all of its fields to create other leaders."

I Art Cleveland is "a youth-serving nonprofit organization promoting access to art education to northeast Ohio youth who do not have full access to art programming outside of their school classrooms." It provides community education about the importance of the arts and awareness about access to arts in the area. I Art Cleveland's programming connects underserved youth to partnering organizations. The final initiative is to provide funding for these same youth to attend local and national arts programs.

The nonprofit also purchases tickets to various arts events, classes, and workshops. It gives the tickets to families to encourage them to attend arts events in Cleveland.

Talking about I Art Cleveland is bittersweet for Kynnedy. She considers the organization one of her biggest successes and one of her biggest failures. She acknowledges that she was young and inexperienced when she started it.

> **There was a lot more I could have done with the organization if I really understood more about nonprofit management. I am learning more now.**

Kynnedy is now working on creating more initiatives and partnerships for I Art Cleveland. She is optimistic that the organization is going in a new, more efficient direction. She even wants to expand it to have hubs in different cities.

Chat(Her) Talks

After attending Disney Dreamers Academy, Kynnedy was inspired to start her second initiative, called Chat(Her) Talks, an "online forum that gives all girls a seat at the table and creates a safe space for them to connect and inspire." Kynnedy started the forum to promote sisterhood and community. Any person using she/her/hers or they/them/their pronouns can participate in Chat(Her).

Chat(Her) has covered topics on self-care, entrepreneurship, community leadership, college prep, politics, and STEM, to name a few. One speaker series was called, "We Have Spoken & Protested. Now What? Future Action Steps for Young Social Activists." It featured a discussion encouraging youth to become civic and community leaders in the wake of political and social unrest.

Kynnedy started Chat(Her) so she could share her community with others. She works on the initiative with a team of other young Black women, all accomplished teenagers and community leaders with a passion to empower and change the lives of other girls. Kynnedy wants to expand Chat(Her) to include mentoring, coaching, and eventually a larger summit.

She is in the process of obtaining a 501(c)(3) status for the organization. As with I Art Cleveland, Kynnedy wants Chat(Her) to become a national and worldwide initiative.

Kynnedy is intentional about her work. Her overall goal is to combine her interests in music, activism, arts, and STEM—an objective that is clear in all of her organizational efforts. She sets high standards for herself and those who work alongside her.

> " I believe in speaking things into the universe. I am really big on manifesting. Manifesting power and peace for myself and my friends and family. "

Kynnedy has reaped the rewards of her commitment to daily affirmations, positive thinking, and hard work. At the same time, Kynnedy knows that life is not formulaic. It has ups and downs and unpredictable twists that we can neither control nor predict. Yet, though we may not be in complete control, we can commit ourselves to getting the most out of the lives we have been blessed with.

Kynnedy received a full, four-year scholarship from QuestBridge. She's on track to graduate from Columbia University in 2025 with a BS in Computer Science. She wants to be able to explore her artistry and her tech side, because one of her long-term goals is to create a tech company whose products cater to underrepresented communities.

What we can learn from
KYNNEDY SIMONE SMITH

PACESETTING LEADERSHIP

The pacesetting leader is high achieving. They are usually self-motivated trendsetters who take initiative and clearly communicate requirements. But even though Kynnedy has high expectations for success and performance, she is willing to step aside and let others manifest their leadership. How can you set goals and be a strong leader while still allowing others to lead as well?

TAKE THINGS STEP-BY-STEP

Kynnedy reminds herself to take things step-by-step, stay within a framework that she can manage, and try not to overwhelm herself with tasks. This can be difficult for high achievers who take on so much. But there are lessons to be learned on any journey, and when we take things one step at a time, we can take advantage of all of the teachable moments that come during the journey.

THE IMPORTANCE OF SISTERHOOD

In ten years, Kynnedy says she wants to "have a community of sisterhood." For young Black women often on the margins of society, Black sisterhood is especially important for identity and survival. Black women and girls need each other simply because it is crucial for us to thrive. We need spaces where we can be our most authentic selves. There is power in sisterhood.

LEARN FROM YOUR MISTAKES

While Kynnedy is a successful young woman, she spent time reflecting on her failures so she could learn from those experiences to better herself. Kynnedy learned to channel those experiences of failure into teachable moments. What was something you failed at that you can now use to learn from?

> " **When I was 14 years old, my own experiences with misogynoir and the grief that comes from seeing police murdering Black people galvanized me into the work that I do.** "

Stephanie Younger, Founder of
Black Feminist Collective

STANDING WITH THE PEOPLE: THE AGENCY OF STEPHANIE YOUNGER

8

Once upon a time, Stephanie Younger was too shy to speak in public. As a child, she was often quiet and withdrawn. Though her words never managed to flow confidently, her sharp mind always found a way to process the world around her through a critical lens.

It wasn't until Stephanie began working with the Richmond Youth Peace Project that she overcame her fear of public speaking. In response to police violence against Black people, Stephanie started performing spoken word poetry. In one performance, she stood at the mic in the center of the stage. Her plain clothes allowed the audience to focus on her youthful face and quiet yet penetrating voice.

Stephanie told the story of a young Black person who gets shot late at night at a gas station when an officer stops them in a suburban neighborhood. In her poem, Stephanie speaks directly to the victim:

"Let your last words be, 'Black lives matter. My life matters.'"

On any given day, Stephanie can be found at a rally, speaking boldly in front of crowds and protesting injustices.

Stephanie says that she internalized misogynoir from age 6 to 12. *Misogynoir* is "the specific hatred, dislike, distrust, and prejudice directed toward Black women." This is a word Stephanie uses often to describe her personal journey. She has many stories of traumatic racial incidents during her adolescence, the majority of which took place within her school system in central Virginia.

"I remember my teacher often accused me of being physically aggressive toward other people. I remember being brought to the principal's office when I had a panic attack during a storm at school. I remember being accused of cheating for no reason. I remember these instances, but I never thought much of them until recently."

Typically, people do not have many memories from early childhood. But in Stephanie's case, her experiences were painful enough that she can recall almost every detail.

One afternoon, while Stephanie was on the monkey bars at the playground, a group of girls laughed and called her a monkey. Stephanie told her mother, who spoke with Stephanie's teacher about it. The teacher quickly excused the girls, saying, "Oh no, we just read a book about monkeys, so it's okay."

INTERSECTIONALITY

Kimberlé Williams Crenshaw is a prominent scholar who focuses her work on civil rights, Black feminist legal theory, and critical race theory. She is responsible for originating the word *intersectionality*, which the Oxford English Dictionary defines as "the interconnected nature of social categorizations such as race, class, and gender, regarded as creating overlapping and interdependent systems of discrimination or disadvantage." The term suggests that people are often oppressed by multiple layers of their identity, which can include race, gender, sexual orientation, and other spheres.

Black Feminist Collective

The 2016 presidential election of Donald Trump led to a cultural awakening and ignited a women's movement.

"I had just recently learned what feminism was," Stephanie says. "I actually learned what intersectionality was days after Trump was elected. Unfortunate with the timing."

Stephanie attended the Women's March that took place after Trump's inauguration. But she did not quite understand her role as a Black person and Black woman in the midst of the societal change. While that moment in early 2017 began a personal exploration for Stephanie, it was the previous summer that changed the way she saw the world. In July 2016, the shooting deaths of Alton Sterling in Louisiana and Philando Castile in Minnesota led to protests across the country.

> **❝ Seeing the news coverage of Black people being murdered by the police, I was conflicted over what I should advocate for. Should I advocate for the interests of my race or should I advocate for the interests of my gender? ❞**

Stephanie came to the realization that she should not just advocate for the interests of Black men and white women; she should be advocating for Black women and girls as well.

"Being Black and female is not mutually exclusive," she says.

Words are important to Stephanie. One day, she decided to use her words to write about the importance of centering the work and voices of Black women and girls. She created a website as a platform to post an article dedicated to highlighting that intersectionality. The article was titled, "14 Black Girls, Women & Nonbinary People Every Womanist Should Know About." Within days, the post went viral and was read by tens of thousands of people. Stephanie was only 14 years old at the time. In the article, she wrote:

"Many institutions fail to educate people about Black liberation and the feminist movement from the narratives [of] Black women, Black girls, and Black nonbinary people, who are often discredited for their work on the front lines of Black liberation—which is often centered around cis[gender] het[erosexual] Black men, and mainstream feminism—which often centers cishet white women . . . I am grateful [to] be part of a generation where Kimberle Crenshaw's theory of intersectionality, Alice Walker's definition of womanism, and other movements led by Black feminists are building a socially and politically just society."

Stephanie called the site where she posted the article "Black Feminist Collective." She used the attention her article had received

Black Feminist Collective has more than sixty contributing authors who write about Black liberation, intersectionality, womanism, and other similar topics. These authors are from the United States, Latin America, and various countries in Africa and East Asia.

Stephanie has not only written opinion pieces but has also interviewed notable activists to highlight their work. She has been thinking about making Black Feminist Collective into an organization and wondering how she can move it beyond writing and virtual activism.

Meanwhile, Stephanie's personal activism has extended beyond her virtual platform as she has gotten more involved in community organizing and training. In addition to attending protests, Stephanie has also worked with the Richmond Youth Peace Project, a Richmond Peace Education Center program that teaches, among other things, conflict resolution, leadership training, peace, and social justice through the arts. In the three years she was with the project, Stephanie worked with other young people on how to apply nonviolent conflict resolution.

66 **Even when I have conflicts with myself as a person, conflict resolution is a great tool for self-care and for de-escalation with other people.** 99

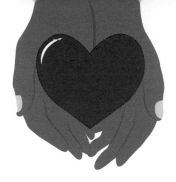

Stephanie is also an advocate for juvenile justice reform and gun violence prevention. She has been involved in the Virginia Youth Climate Cooperative, Youth Climate Strikes, and the American Civil Liberties Union. She has continued to participate in and organize rallies.

Stephanie is most proud of her involvement in the Rise for Youth organization, a "nonpartisan campaign in support of community alternatives to youth incarceration." She has been with the organization for years now. After one of her performances, she was invited to a screening of the documentary *Free Angela and All Political Prisoners*. The film is about the social activism of political activist, academic, and author Angela Davis.

At the event, Stephanie was inspired by Davis's work and even had an opportunity to speak with her. This experience thrust Stephanie into new work advocating for the abolishment of prisons. Fighting and advocating for multiple causes may sound like a daunting and overwhelming life to lead, but to Stephanie, this lifestyle is the norm for Black women.

" People often forget that Black Lives Matter was started by three Black women. [They are all] queer Black women. Black women led liberation movements. Black women [are] leading the climate strikes. Fighting for gun violence. We've been doing this for generations. "

What we can learn from
STEPHANIE YOUNGER

AUTONOMOUS LEADERSHIP

Because of her early experiences with racial trauma, Stephanie felt powerless as a young girl. She has since taken that power back, expressing it through her personal agency in her work. Stephanie now recognizes that she has the power to influence her own thoughts and actions. She has taken control over her own life and circumstances. What can you do to more positively influence your own thoughts and actions?

WORDS MATTER

Words had a tremendous effect on Stephanie as a child. Her painful experiences were the result of racist and misogynistic words spoken to her. But hearing words like "Black is beautiful" helped Stephanie erase the negative stigma associated with Blackness. We can be intentional about the words we speak to ourselves and others, and we can choose to use words that lift up rather than tear down.

CREATE YOUR OWN PLATFORM

Black Feminist Collective emerged because Stephanie had a message she wanted to get out. She then put pen to paper and wrote an article highlighting Black women, girls, and non-binary people who are doing important work in society. Instead of pitching her article to a site, she created her own site. Sometimes, the best way to make sure your message is heard is to create your own platform to share it.

BE AN ADVOCATE

"One of the biggest parts of being a leader, especially when it comes to activism and justice work, is to stand with people," Stephanie says. "Everyone has a voice that deserves to be uplifted." Stephanie knows what it was like to have no one standing up for her when she needed an advocate most. Like Stephanie, we can use our platforms and spheres of influence to speak on behalf of and for the liberation of the oppressed.

"**If they don't give you a seat at the table, bring a folding chair.**"

Shirley Chisholm

CONCLUSION

BLACK HERITAGE

SHIRLEY CHISHOLM

2014

In 1972, Shirley Chisholm became the first woman and first Black major-party candidate to run for president of the United States. Her campaign message was "Unbought & Unbossed." Fifty years later, young Black girls are following in her legacy with their leadership, resilience, and integrity. They, too, are showing the world that they are unbossed.

The girls whose stories and leadership were shared in this book all have unique experiences, vary in age, and come from different backgrounds. What they do share, however, is their sheer will, desire, and passion to turn unfortunate circumstances into something hopeful. They use their influence and platforms to create and sustain social change and bring awareness to injustice. They use their God-given gifts to make the world a better place.

Because of them, I am more hopeful.